Marina

Conserving the Rain Forest

by Elzira Guzman

HOUGHTON MIFFLIN   BOSTON

Marina's Home

Marina Silva talks about things that are important to the people where she lives.

Marina Silva grew up near the Amazon River, so she is called a daughter of the Amazon. Today, she works to protect this area and the people who live there. She is the leader of the peoples of the jungle.

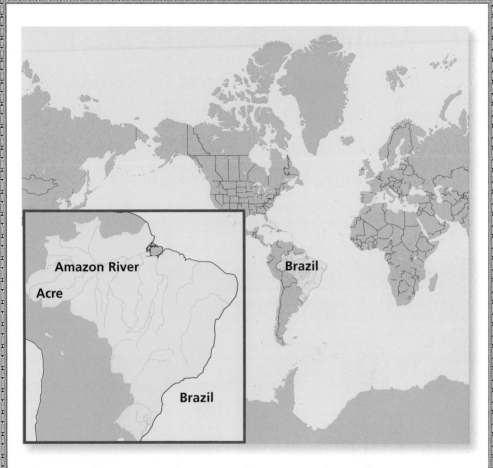

The smaller map shows where Marina Silva comes from.

Marina Silva was born in a country in South America called Brazil. She grew up in an area near the Amazon River. Her home state of Acre is part of the Amazon Rain Forest.

3

Animals in the Rain Forest

In the Amazon Rain Forest, trees crowd together. Other plants and flowers grow thick and full. Birds call and insects hum. Many other kinds of animals swing through the trees or run through the forest.

Frog

Butterfly

The Amazon Rain Forest is rich with plants and animals. In fact, it is the home of several million kinds of plants, birds, and insects. Some of these are found nowhere else on Earth.

Sloth

Grasshopper

People in the Rain Forest

This boy paddles a canoe down the Amazon River.

The Amazon Rain Forest is also the home of a certain group of people. Their way of life depends on the rain forest. It is their source of food, work, and pleasure. But each year, people cut down trees. There is less and less rain forest left.

People cut down trees in this area of the Amazon.

Marina Silva wants to prevent the rain forest from being destroyed. "When I fly over the Amazon by plane, I love to look at the green carpet of forest, crisscrossed by rivers," Silva said. She said that she feels pain when she sees an area that has been cut down.

Collecting Rubber

Rubber is collected from trees in the rain forest.

Her love of the rain forest began at an early age. As a young girl, Silva worked in the jungle with her father. Her father was a seringueiro (SAY reen gway roh), or a person who gathers rubber from rubber trees. Another name for this job is rubber tapper.

Marina Silva visits an area where people get rubber.

To do this job, Silva would wake up early in the morning. She and her father would walk many miles through the rain forest each day. To get the rubber, rubber tappers use a sharp knife to cut the tree bark. The white liquid rubber flows from the tree. Rubber tappers gather it, weigh it, and sell it. Later the liquid is made into other things, such as car tires or the soles of shoes.

Going to School

Silva did not go to school. There were no schools in her area. She did not know how to read or write. Her main job was helping her father support their large family.

The work was long and difficult. But there came a time in her teens when Silva was not able to help. She became ill.

"I was unable to do the heavy rubber-tapping work," she says. "I asked my father if I could move to the city because I wanted to study."

So Silva went to school. She moved to the city of Rio Branco to get treatment for her illness. While there, she went to school. Silva learned all the skills she had missed in earlier years. In just three years, Silva graduated from the university where she studied history.

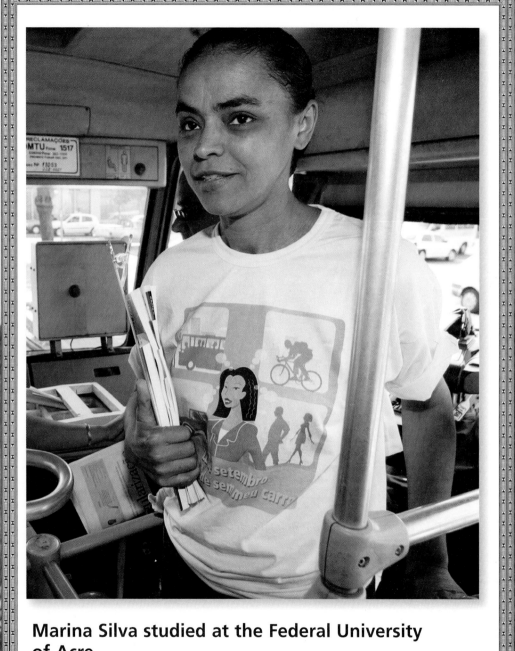

Marina Silva studied at the Federal University of Acre.

Oxygen Cycle

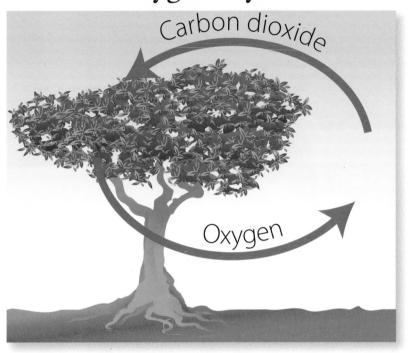

Carbon dioxide

Oxygen

Silva also learned about the importance of the rain forest. It is important not only to the people of Brazil but to the whole world. It is a unique area. Its many plants help make oxygen, a gas that people need to breathe. The plants use another gas, carbon dioxide. If that gas is not used, it could build up and cause a change in the climate.

Helping People

Chico Mendes worked with Marina Silva.

In the city, Silva met a man named Chico Mendes. Mendes was working for the rights of the people of the rain forest. He wanted to help rubber tappers and other rain forest workers. Silva believed in these causes. She worked alongside Mendes. Sadly, Mendes was killed by people who were against his causes.

Saving the Forest

Marina Silva speaks about protecting the rain forest.

Silva continued the work, though. In the mid-1990s, she ran for senator in Brazil's government. She was elected by the people. At the age of 36, Silva was the youngest senator ever in Brazil. She worked to get laws passed to protect the rain forest and the people who live there. Silva has been honored with several awards.

Some farmers cut and burn trees and plants in the Amazon.

In 2003, Silva became Brazil's minister of the environment. In this job, she continues her work for the rain forest and its people. Silva explains that there must be a balance between the traditional ways of the rain forest people and the modern ways of doing things.

There is one thing that Silva would especially like to see change about the rain forest. That is the way that some Amazon farmers cut down an area of trees, burn all the plants on the land, and then plant crops so that the rain forest disappears.

Marina Silva has been thanked for her work.

Change will not be easy, but Silva plans to work with the rain forest people and the government to do what is best.

"They say I am a fighter," Silva has said. "I agree, but I think that, in myself, the fight comes after the dream."